Responsible Innovation

RESPONSIBLE INNOVATION

Philippe de Woot

Greenleaf
PUBLISHING

Published by
Greenleaf Publishing Limited
Aizlewood's Mill, Nursery Street
Sheffield S3 8GG, UK
www.greenleaf-publishing.com

Printed and bound by Printondemand-worldwide.com, UK

Cover by Sadie Gornall-Jones
Copy-editing and typesetting by Andrew Welsh (www.andrew-welsh.com)

British Library Cataloguing in Publication Data:
A catalogue record for this book is available from the British Library.
ISBN-13: 978-1-78353-443-2 [paperback]
ISBN-13: 978-1-78353-521-7 [hardback]
ISBN-13: 978-1-78353-439-5 [PDF ebook]
ISBN-13: 978-1-78353-441-8 [ePub ebook]

Original edition: *L'innovation, moteur de l'économie,* L'Académie en Poche; Académie Royale de Belgique, 2014

The problem that is usually being considered is how capitalism administers existing structures,
whereas the relevant problem is how it creates and destroys them.

(Schumpeter)

A change always lays the cornerstone for a new change.

(Machiavelli)

For those who spread their sails in the right way to the winds of the earth will always find themselves borne by a current toward the open seas.

(Teilhard de Chardin)

Man cannot discover new oceans unless he has the courage to lose sight of the shore.

(Gide)

We have gone further than we thought because we have been innovative.

(Eric Domb)

The new, barely born, is soon an old moon.

(Jean d'Ormesson)

Contents

Introduction

Economic development is rooted in rupture and not in equilibrium. The competition that really counts is competition by innovation, applied to existing products and services. It does not have a marginal role but is central to progress. This type of competition acts through creative destruction.

The agent of this competitive struggle is an unusual character: the entrepreneur. He has very specific qualities that are rarely combined in an individual: **vision** of potential progress; a sufficient **appetite for risk** and a determination to implement; and an **energy** and **power of conviction** to bring about the necessary assistance and resources.

Today, enterprises themselves play the role of innovator. They have become "collective entrepreneurs".

If successful companies are observed over a period of five to ten years, not one of them has failed to adapt, transform, renew. All have evolved, and all have innovated in their products, in their markets or in their processes and their organization. Under the pressure of competition, the company is obliged to adopt this logic of innovation, creativity and change. Its long-term survival depends on it.

The reason for this is that it gives the enterprise a decisive lead and a major comparative advantage; this innovation is the competitive weapon par excellence, providing a sort of temporary monopoly. This allows the company to set high prices and often reap significant profit, which then finance the conquest of markets, rapid growth, the development of new innovations or the acquisition of faster innovators.

By becoming collective, entrepreneurial qualities have grown considerably. The company has become an entrepreneur with enhanced capacities. Its power is increasing and it controls and directs key development resources: scientific and technological knowledge, managerial and organizational skills, innovative partnerships, information networks and influence… Its ability to innovate is raised to the level of a global economy. This enhanced capacity allows the enterprise to better face the challenges of the 21st century, but it also accentuates its breaking and destructive power.

Innovation acts as a powerful engine of economic development. Is it always for the common good? The dark side of this extraordinary dynamism lies precisely in its destructive power. If simply left to market forces, it might cause social havoc and great human suffering. Another issue is that scientific and technical creativity is sometimes very ambiguous in its applications. Given its acceleration, we will need to manage its development from a more ethical and societal perspective.

This power is becoming more independent. Globally, companies act in an almost complete political vacuum. Economic globalization is advancing much faster than its necessary governance and regulation. It is escaping the realm of nation states and gradually imposing its logic on the whole world.[1] This failure of politics to catch up with economics leads to a kind of public powerlessness to drive genuine development strategies and democratically discuss the social ramifications of technological advances. Economic creativity also operates in an ethical vacuum. The market economy operates on a logic of means and not a logic of ends: it aims to maximize the creation and use of scarce resources and the

---

1 See B. Frydman, *La fabrique de normes* (Académie en Poche, 2014).

benefits that result therefrom. It is based on technical, managerial and financial modernity and not on values. This system is amoral. It does not contain any measures other than that of solvent markets.

A central theme of this book is that entrepreneurship, creativity and innovation are needed to face the global challenges of our time. Although the existing business model is the source of major malfunctions, the enterprise, in the broadest sense, can help address many of them. A **problem** can become a **solution**.

This is where the true social responsibility of the entrepreneur lies. It is through creativity that he may serve the common good. It is important to rethink the direction of his creative power and his ability to correct the excesses of the system he runs. A responsible innovator can contribute, with others, to solving the global problems of the 21st century. In many areas, he has already begun to do that. Do not underestimate the potentially beneficial power of innovation.

At the scale of a country or group of countries, the development of entrepreneurship across society is only possible if the environment is favourable. It is a complex problem because it is affected by the outlook and the very culture of society. Entrepreneurship is not decreed but can be encouraged through the creation of favourable conditions for its emergence. These conditions are many and they are interdependent:

academic density and openness; skills clusters in the sectors of the future; cohabitation of global companies; innovative small and medium-sized enterprises (SMEs) and individual entrepreneurs; financing facilities; administrative and institutional simplicity; attitude towards business, risk and success; tolerance of failure... If one of these elements is weak, it weakens the whole entrepreneurial fabric of the country.

While we are better aware today that the conventional theoretical foundations of our economic system describe its practical application only very imperfectly,[2] it is generally agreed that the entrepreneurial theory gives a fairly realistic description. However, economic theory should better take into account competition by innovation, the creativity of the company, and its power and responsibilities. It should also meet its ethical and political dimensions. As long as the theory continues to gives more importance to equilibrium than to rupture, its analysis will be incomplete, and its recommendations ineffective.

---

2 See the discussion on the realism of economic theory in J.P. Hansen, *La vraie nature du marché* (De Boeck, 2012). See also S. Keen, *Debunking Economics* (Zed Books, 2011); B. Colmant and P. Jorion, *Penser l'économie autrement* (Fayard, 2014). Other economists follow this view. Stiglitz claims that economic theory has become a self-sufficient world giving a false depiction of reality. Amartya Sen adds that "homo œconomicus" is a rational idiot.

The Holy Grail of economic equity[3] will be found less in a "general equilibrium" and more in better focused creativity and a more responsible entrepreneurship. If we want more realistic economic analysis, it is necessary to put innovation at the centre of the debate. As a human science, economics should not limit the analysis to the best use of scarce resources but should try to better understand and explain the creation of material progress and its consequences for society.

3   See J.P. Hansen, *Une quête de Graal. La recherche de l'équité en environnement économique* (Académie en Poche, 2014).

1
Innovation at the heart of the economy

The decisive competitive weapon

The foundations of economic development are innovations, ruptures and destruction. Classical economic theory has sought to ascertain the existence of a general balance in which competition sets the rules of the game through the famous invisible hand. For this, competition focuses on price levels and production volumes. It is through these mechanisms that supply and demand adjusts, sector by sector, pushing everything towards equilibrium. This theory proceeds "in a given state of technique and organization"[4] and does not take into account innovation or the imbalances it causes. It took Schumpeter (1883–1950) to show that innovation is more important than price and that the movement, rupture and destruction inherent in competitive models, the constantly disturbed equilibrium, could never be more than a trend. If we want the economic and policy analysis that results to be more realistic, it is necessary to put innovation at the centre of the debate.[5]

> The competition that really matters is the competition of new goods, new techniques, new sources, new kinds of organization (the control of larger units, for example); competition which commands a decisive cost advantage or quality that affects not just the profit margin or the quantities produced by existing firms, but their foundations and their very existence. This form of competition is much more effective, in the same way as a bombardment is more effective than merely forcing a door. It is so much more significant that it becomes relatively indifferent to whether or not competition, in the

4 L.H. Dupriez, *Philosophie des conjonctures économiques* (Nauwelaerts, 1959).
5 Today, Schumpeter's approach is not always well integrated into a general theory that, based on marginalism, relates poorly to the ruptures inherent to the functioning of the economy.

ordinary sense, functions more or less prompt-
ly; the powerful lever which, in the long run,
increases production and lowers the price, is
exerted in a different way. The problem that is
generally considered is how capitalism facili-
tates existing structures, while the major issue
is to discover how it creates and then destroys
these structures.[6]

Schumpeter added, "This process of creative destruction is the fundamental fact of capitalism. This is the
essence of capitalism, and every capitalist enterprise
must, whether they like it or not, adapt".[7]

From this perspective, economic development is
mainly achieved by innovation, and the agent of this
is an extraordinary personality: the entrepreneur.
The entrepreneur is a rare personality that has very
specific qualities that are rarely combined in a sin-
gle individual: the vision of possible progress, a sufficient **taste for risk** to implement, and the **energy
and power of conviction** to obtain the necessary
support and resources. The innovative entrepreneur,
through their creativity, transforms the nature of
competition. Enterprise, instead of being limited to

6 J. Schumpeter, *The Theory of Economic Development*
(Cambridge, MA: Harvard University Press, 1949).
7 J. Schumpeter, *Capitalism, Socialism and Democracy*
(Allen and Unwin, 1944).

mere price wars, is actually a race for innovation and technical progress.

The scientific and technical advances and changes those impose on society are not new. They are a part of human history. Since prehistoric times, technical innovations have represented the milestones of our evolution: Palaeolithic, Neolithic, Bronze Age, Iron Age... The transformations of our expertise are seen as major changes for society: stock-breeding, agriculture, writing, printing, ocean navigation, digital... and the Internet. Since the Industrial Revolution, the great stages of economic development have not been represented by price changes but by technical advances: steam engines, railways, electricity, the combustion engine, electronics, biotechnology... It therefore seems difficult to avoid putting innovation at the centre of economic theory, and to reduce the theory to a simple set of prices and quantities produced.

At the end of his life, Schumpeter seemed to believe that the specific role of the entrepreneur was becoming increasingly useless. His view was that, with progress being mechanized, innovation will be replaced with routine and any vision of potential progress will be replaced by calculation; there would be no more resistance to change, and the energy to overcome it would have no *raison d'être*. However, new barriers to innovation will arise without the entrepreneur having any control over them: social forces, official price controls, the hostility of government bureaucracy...

We know that this has not been the case. On the contrary, the pace of innovation has accelerated, entrepreneurial capabilities have greatly developed, and routine has not replaced creative initiative. But today entrepreneurial drive is no longer the exclusive prerogative of the individual innovator. This drive has become more collective, and businesses, to some extent, have taken over from individual entrepreneurs. Innovation may be more systematic but its destructive power has not stopped growing.

The collective entrepreneur: increased innovative power

Individual entrepreneurs are atypical and rare personalities. Essentially non-conformist, the entrepreneur–innovator is described as "very visionary", "bubbling inside", a "taboo-breaker", operating "out of the comfort zone", "inhabited by a passion", "never giving up", "working one hundred hours a week", "demanding, iconoclastic, obsessed with the long term", "believing that everything he imagines is probably doable". These individual entrepreneurs still call themselves "rebels", "breaking with the single-track thoughts of the sector", "crazy lovers of great challenges", "transforming the unimaginable into reality", "ready to shoot the moon ('moonshots')", "somewhat players", "realisers of their dreams"...[8] They have ultimate confidence in themselves[9] and are not afraid to "take giant steps".

Some of them are even "serial" entrepreneurs. Elon Musk, for example, has successively created Zip 2 (an online directory), PayPal (an online payment service), Tesla (an electric car), SpaceX (a space transport service), Solar City (solar energy systems) and Hyperloop (a propelled capsule on a cushion

---

8 The Pairi Daiza zoological, botanical and cultural park was the childhood dream of its creator, Eric Domb. He describes his dream by the definition that Benoit-Méchin puts forward for gardens: "The great art of the garden is that by which a civilisation seeks not precisely to copy nature but to appropriate the elements it provides to express its highest concept of happiness" (Aset, June 2014). It is interesting to note that businesses also recognise the importance of dreams. The co-founder of Google, Sergey Brin, declared that "Google's dream is to use the latest electronic miniaturisation technology to help improve the life of millions of people".

9 In 2006, in Washington, at a congress of world experts in the space field, an unknown person took the floor: "Hello everyone, my name's Elon Musk. I am the founder of SpaceX. In five years, you will be dead." Today he's in the process of showing his strength. (Cited by D. Gallois, *Le Monde*, 16 August 2014.)

of air inside a tube elevated above the motorway). Richard Branson set up Virgin Records, the airline Virgin Atlantic and the Virgin Galactic space tourism agency. Bertrand Piccard is the initiator of Breitling Orbiter projects (non-stop round-the-world balloons) and Solar Impulse (a solar plane). There is also Steve Jobs, Apple's creator, Mark Zuckerberg, the creator of Facebook, and Larry Page, the founder of Google.

Belgium has a long entrepreneurial tradition. Since the late Middle Ages, its towns were cradles of commercial, industrial and financial innovation, a tradition lauded by historians.10 In the 19th century, after Great Britain, Belgium took the lead in the Industrial Revolution on the continent. This was conducted over more than a century by leading entrepreneurs such as John Cockerill, Gustave Boël, André Dumont, Ernest Solvay, Évence Coppée, Édouard-Louis Empain, Émile Francqui, Jean Jadot, Léon-Léandre Bekaert

10 See in particular H. Pirenne, *Histoire économique et sociale du moyen-âge* (PUF, 1963); F. Braudel, *Civilisation matérielle, économie et capitalisme XVe-XVIIe siècle* (Armand Colin, 1979); H. Hasquin, *Louis XIV face à l'Europe du Nord* (Racine, 2005); R. Kurgan, *100 grands patrons du XXe siècle en Belgique* (Alain Renier, 1999) and *L'innovation technologique, facteur de changement* (Editions de l'ULB, 1986).

and many others such as the wool entrepreneurs of Verviers and the cotton makers of Ghent.[11]

Today, there are still many entrepreneurs in Belgium but they are often in more specialized "niches". For instance, there is Paul Janssen (Janssen Pharmaceutica), Thomas Leysen (Umicore), Jean Stéphenne (RIT and GSK), Laurent Minguet (EVS), Yves Jongen and Pierre Mottet (IBA), Emmanuel Prévinaire (Flying-Cam), Thierry Bogaert (Devgen), Joseph Martial and André Renard (Euro Gentec), Pierre De Muelenaere and Jean-Didier Legat (I.R.I.S.), Jean and José Zurstrassen (Skynet and Keytrade Bank), Didier de Callatay and Godefroid de Wouters (banking and finance software), Eric Domb (Pairi Daiza), Urbain Vandeurzen (LMS), Marc Nolet (PhysiOL) Jean-Jacques Sioen (Sioen Industries), Marc Coucke (Omega Pharma)... University science parks are the start-up incubators in cutting-edge sectors, and there is a host of key players. The main problem is achieving global scale.

A central theme of this book is to show that it is not only the individual entrepreneur who creates innovation.[12] Companies now provide economic

---

11 Simonis, Peltzer and Zurstrassen in Verviers and Braun in Ghent have been the key entrepreneurs in this industry.

12 As is shown by the Louvain School: L. Dupriez, *Des mouvements économiques généraux* (Louvain: Nauwelaerts,

creativity in a collective and systematic manner. To survive in the long term, the company has become a **collective entrepreneur**. The reality of economic and technical development is that major innovations are often first implemented by individual entrepreneurs, and then swiftly adopted, expanded and developed by collective entrepreneurs that are companies. The names Ford, Campbell, Nestlé, Solvay, Bekaert, Lafarge, Michelin, Renault, Dassault, Tata and Honda no longer refer to the individual entrepreneurs who founded them but to the companies that have developed the same qualities of vision, boldness and conviction as their illustrious founders. The most recent examples confirm this reality. Formidable individual entrepreneurs such as Steve Jobs, Bill Gates, Larry Page, Mark Zuckerberg and Elon Musk have quickly transformed into collective entrepreneurs under

1949); *Philosophie des conjonctures économiques* (Louvain: Nauwelaerts, 1959); A. Taymans, *L'homme, agent du développement économique* (Louvain: Nauwelaerts, 1951); P. de Woot, *La fonction d'entreprise* (Louvain: Nauwelaerts, 1962); A. Jacquemin, *L'entreprise et son pouvoir de marché* (PUF, 1967); P. de Woot and X. Desclée, *Le management stratégique des groupes européens* (Paris : Economica, 1984); J.J. Lambin, *Quel avenir pour le capitalisme?* (Dunod, 2011) and *Rethinking the Market Economy* (Palgrave Macmillan, 2014).

the names Apple, Microsoft, Google, Facebook and Tesla, respectively.

The company thus takes the baton from the original innovator and tends to multiply its creative capacity. It can only survive by innovating. Driven by competition and technological developments, a high-performing company not only produces and distributes goods and services but is constantly renewed, evolved and created anew. If successful companies are observed over a period of five or ten years, their key characteristic is that they have adapted, transformed and renewed. All have evolved and all have innovated, either in their products or in their markets or in their processes or organization. The intensity and pace of this renewal will obviously vary from one sector to another but no company subject to competition can stop being creative or it will run the risk of disappearing. In a market economy system, the enterprise is the very agent of economic and technical progress. The enterprise drives that progress and leads it to its most concrete form. It does not just imagine or describe innovation, it makes it happen, it creates.[13]

---

13 It is significant that the *Littré* (a 19th century French dictionary) defines enterprise as "the execution of a project". In echo, General Electric, the American giant, declares: "What we imagine, we can make happen".

Whether we are dealing with breakthrough innovations (new technology, new products, etc.) or incremental innovations (increasing the quality of products and creating the top of the range),[14] this is where the competitive advantage of high-wage countries with strong currencies lies.

Is there an economic sector that has remained motionless without declining or disappearing? All successful economies have been creative and they are all constantly transformed. As previously discussed, innovation is not necessarily technical. It may result from a new organization or a new concept. The example of distribution illustrates this well. In less than 50 years, we have seen the most varied forms of distribution emerge: convenience stores, department stores, supermarkets, hypermarkets, discount stores, shopping centres, specialized shops, e-commerce and, tomorrow, distribution drones. In the field of catering, innovations by McDonald's and Burger King introduced the new concept of fast food. In the field of holidays, innovation has come up with new

14 For a conceptual and philosophical discussion of innovation, see the works of Luc de Brabandère and Anne Mikolajczak, in particular: *Pensée magique, pensée logique: petite philosophie de la créativité* (Le Pommier, 2008) and *Les Mots et les Choses de l'entreprise: approche philosophique de la stratégie et de l'innovation* (Mols, 2012).

deals: Club Méditerranée, boat cruises, Airbnb... We should also mention the example of Pairi Daiza: its creator, Eric Domb, transformed the concept of a zoo into an animal, floral and cultural park; without this new vision, it would not have become Belgium's leading tourist destination and probably would not have got the Chinese pandas denied to most traditional zoos. The transformation, by Benoît Coppée, of the Libramont Fair, a useful centre for the dissemination of innovation in the agricultural world, is relevant to this type of vision. The agricultural sector is not immune to this innovation imperative: after intensive agriculture has developed out of chemical innovations, it now seems on the verge of a revolution. Today, we see a new dawn for agriculture that is based on a better knowledge of soils, no-till, moisture management, and innovative ways of stabling, etc. The revival of a bankrupt company often depends on entrepreneurial initiative, as demonstrated by the creation of Brussels Airlines by Etienne Davignon and Maurice Lippens.

By becoming collective, the entrepreneurial qualities of **vision**, **risk appetite**, and **energy and conviction** have grown considerably. The company has become an entrepreneur with multiplied creative power. Its ability to innovate is raised to the level of a global economy, making it more suitable for the challenges of the 21st century. However, this ability also increases its destructive power.

•   **The vision of possible progress** is systemized and amplified significantly through scientific research. Science has experienced an unprecedented acceleration over the last century, with several factors contributing to this: the accumulation of knowledge and its rapid spread has opened up broader and more ambitious fields of investigation to researchers; the intersection of disciplines and universal access to information has fostered new and bolder research; and technological competition that has become global has strengthened the movement and multiplied the means of funding for research and development. The intensity of research within a company obviously varies from one sector to another, ranging from 5% of turnover in the automotive industry to 20% in the pharmaceutical industry. In 2014, Bayer spent €3.2 billion in research and development in the life sciences; 13,000 people are working in this department. By mastering scientific methods and tools, the company has put the power of knowledge at the service of its economic strategies. Techno-science constantly offers the company new opportunities for innovation and more powerful competitive weapons. It is the company that transforms, often as they emerge, scientific knowledge and technologies into products and services.[15] In so doing, it has greatly accelerated the transition of scientific discovery and technical innovation to commercial exploitation.[16] Some Internet giants do not hesitate to hire the best researchers and to cross-reference their knowledge to better prepare for the future.

• **The appetite for risk** and the ability to take risks also become a collective reality. Economic creation is often achieved through huge bets. One example, among others, is the recent investments by European telecommunications operators for third-generation (3G) and fourth-generation (4G) very high mobile frequencies, which amounted to more than €100 billion for obtaining licenses.

15 "Are genetics the medicine of the XXI century? While scientists are barely sketching out the first responses, start-ups and large laboratories are in the starting-blocks. In 2014, the sequencing and genetic testing market was already worth 20 billion dollars with constantly expanding applications." (H. Hecketsweiler, "Le business en or de l'ADN", *Le Monde*, 2 September 2014).

16 This passage lasted 112 years for photography, 56 for telephony, 36 for radio, 15 for radar, 12 for television, 6 for the atom, 3 for solar batteries, and a few months for the new generations of electronic components.

Added to this are the tens of billions more euros required for infrastructure. Today, no one can say how long it will take to amortize these huge amounts, and 5G is already on its way! Another example is the new EPR type of nuclear reactor under construction at Flamanville: it will cost EDF €9 billion, or three times the price originally planned.

Innovation is, by its nature, risky. Many innovations are constantly emerging, but not all are sustainable successes. The time-frame for acceptance by the market varies greatly from case to case, and the first to start the race is not always the winner. A competitor who starts out later may have the best chance. Americans define successful "competition by innovation" as the ability to enter second in a revolving door and come out first.

The stakes are often at the level of the risks incurred: the area of nano-materials, for example, could represent 300,000–400,000 direct jobs in Europe; shale gas is beginning to make the US energy independent; the sequencing and genetic testing market is estimated at $20 billion; genetically modified organisms (GMOs) could strongly contribute to feeding a world population predicted to reach 9 billion people...

- **The power to initiate and convince** developed accordingly. In these arenas, key players must be powerful, and large multinational companies are increasingly arming themselves to face such risks. Their power is increasing and, in developing these entrepreneurial qualities, companies have become capable of innovative strategies for the long term. They have acquired and developed key resources for creativity: scientific and technological knowledge; managerial and organizational skills; innovative partnerships; information networks and influence... They have become true "strong points" in their field, often capable of remaining sufficiently strong enough to organize their metamorphosis into a new business serving new sectors if theirs is ageing. They retain an entrepreneurial capacity, forge creative partnerships and often buy out start-ups that have innovated faster than they have. By constantly practicing competitive strategies in which innovation is a major component, they become agents of their own development. For example, in 2013, Bosch spent €4.5 billion on research and development and employed 1,200 researchers, complemented by 44,000 engineers in the various business units of the group.

    Such companies are able to attract increasingly significant funding. Often conservative in the distribution of dividends, leading companies can set up a war chest that is able to finance new developments and acquisitions. Google's war chest, for example, amounts to $59 billion, allowing it to buy almost anything that moves in its field and in neighbouring fields. At its zenith, IBM had a net surplus that was 10–20 times larger than those of its major competitors. The market capitalization of Internet champions has reached record levels in recent history.

The ability to convince customers has reached global proportions. For the information and communication industry, for example, it involves convincing tens of millions of customers using broadband networks, TV-on-demand services and Internet applications. In less than ten years, Internet companies have managed to bring together as many users as was achieved in television ownership in 50 years and in radio ownership in over a century.[17] With 800 million iTunes users who have entrusted their credit card number, Apple is able to unite a broad spectrum of the payment industry on its platform and this in turn has led to the implementation of Apple Pay, the

17 S. Salvagio and L. Callis, *Cybersexe* (Ed Luc Pire, 2002).

contactless payment method that is now the dominant innovation in this field.

Racing ahead and temporary monopolies

Under the pressure of competition, companies are obliged to adopt this logic of innovation, creativity and change. Their long-term survival depends on their ability to engage in this race to technical progress and stay for as long as possible in the top ranks of their field. The etymology of the word competition is explicit: run together. Competition is often referred to with phrases such as "stay in the forefront", "start as the first" or "the prime mover", "race to the bottom", "head start", "taking the lead", "racing ahead", etc.

Innovation is the competitive weapon par excellence because it gives the company **a decisive lead and a major comparative advantage**. It provides a sort of temporary monopoly. This allows the company to set high prices and often reap significant profits. These profits then finance the conquest of markets, rapid growth, and the development of new innovations or acquisition of faster innovators to perpetuate the company's growth and secure its position. This temporary monopoly also allows these companies to enter new areas and innovate almost cumulatively. The leading company tries to stay ahead of its industry until it forms an oligopoly or a more innovative competitor dethrones or destroys it. An American adage aptly describes the constant pressure for renewal and the danger of any slowdown: "stop for lunch and you are lunch".

It is in this dynamic that the winning strategies of successful companies lie. The aim of these strategies is for companies to lead the race and stay there. They place, for a time at least, the company in a dominant position. The strongest prevails. But this advance is rarely absolute and is never final.

As the concept of temporary monopoly is the focus of competition by innovation, we will illustrate how it works with concrete examples in order to underscore its influence on the market economy and better depict how its powerful dynamism both drives the economy and continues to unbalance and deconstruct it.

There are numerous examples, such as Bayer with aspirin, Coca-Cola thanks to its "secret" formula, Nestlé with its Nespresso capsules, MacDonald's in fast food, LEGO in construction games, Intel in electronic components, Apple in PCs, Samsung in smartphones, Schlumberger in oil exploration equipment,

Walmart in large out-of-town supermarkets,[18] Sony in gaming consoles and Netflix in streaming.

Information and communication technology has experienced three major waves. There are clear leaders in each category. When **computers** appeared, innovations by IBM allowed it to occupy and long retain over 60% of the global market; for PCs, after a short-lived dominance by IBM, advances were made by Apple and their Macintosh series. For the **software** wave, the Windows operating system boosted Microsoft so much that it was installed on nine out of ten new PCs in the world. As for the wave of **networking** and connectivity, the lead taken by Google through its search engine has made it the undisputed leader on the Internet.[19]

Having become global leaders, these companies have developed, as described above, a true entrepreneurial culture and continuous innovation capacity. This has allowed them to consistently get out of their "comfort zone" and constantly experiment with new products, including products completely out of their original sector. From being a leader in computer

18 Walmart, the world's largest company, currently has 2.2 million employees.
19 In ten years, Google has become the third highest stock market capitalisation, at $391 billion, ahead of Microsoft at $369 billion.

manufacture, IBM has converted into a leader in services and design. Apple has never stopped innovating: smartphones, tablets, connected watches, contactless payment. Microsoft is diversifying into mobile by buying Nokia and has entered "cloud computing"[20] in alliance with Oracle. Google has entered the market for mobile operating systems by buying Android, now the most used system in the world, and the video sector by acquiring YouTube. It is also aiming at the connectivity between houses and objects (glasses, watches, clothing…) and health (the human genome). HP, in order to revive the fixed desktop PC, is launching a major innovation in interaction with a computer that can be used without a keyboard or mouse thanks to a touch surface powered by a DLP projector sending images that can be adjusted.

Pierre-Yves Gomez analyses in fine detail the dynamics of creating leadership through Web champions:[21]

> The digital network economy has exploded the conventional logic of capital accumulation: few employees,[22] little technological capital,

---

20 Decentralised IT in clouds of computers connected by the Internet.
21 P.Y. Gomez, "Facebook, réseau verrouillé", *Le Monde*, 17 March 2014; see also P.Y. Gomez and H. Korin, *L'entreprise dans la démocratie* (De Boeck, 2009).
22 Nevertheless, Facebook employs over 100,000 people.

for a huge number of customers. So Facebook is used by one billion people a month against 39 million customers per month for EDF... The digital network economy grows by aggregating connected users. The more there are, the more they feed into network content, the more they exchange information, data, services and even applications that they develop themselves, the more content becomes attractive to new users. To establish their power, digital companies must always allow more users to connect anywhere. So they buy companies or applications that attract new users. That's why Google has absorbed 125 companies in ten years, including YouTube and Android. Facebook has acquired WhatsApp, a messaging service used by 450 million people. In search of dominance, these companies are start-up hoovers, the purpose being to prevent their network breaking down if producer customers turn away.

The pharmaceutical industry also clearly illustrates the establishment of leadership positions by certain companies and the requirement of those companies to continually innovate to maintain their position. The case of Roche shows that such a strategy, when done well, makes it possible to thrive and survive for several generations. This company has experienced four periods in which real leaderships have been created: in plants in the 19th century, then chemistry, then biotechnology and now in the stem cells that give it leadership in experiments *in vivo*. During the third phase, it took a decisive lead in oncology by acquiring Genentech, which had developed three key drugs for cancer. This gave it 60% of the global market for ten years. In Belgium, UCB ensured its success with niche leaderships where it was the world number one: Zyrtec, an anti-allergic, which was a "blockbuster" (sales exceeding $1 billion per year) and Nootropil for malfunctions of the brain. Today, it is preparing for the next generation by launching innovative medicines in the area of central nervous system and immunological disorders as it seeks new global leaderships. The same applies to GSK and its vaccines, and Janssen Pharmaceutica. Large buy-outs are continuous. Sanofi and MannKind Corporation Medication announced in 2014 that they were entering into a worldwide agreement for the development and commercialization of Afrezza, an inhalable form of insulin. Mega-mergers are designed to strengthen the innovative power of business, and they are often used to find growth drivers and to balance and rejuvenate the product portfolio. This is the case of the recent merger between Allergan (leader of the Botox wrinkle treatment) and Activis (Namenda treatment against Parkinson's and Alzheimer's disease). Roche is preparing to buy the InterMune laboratory specializing in respiratory diseases, and Pfizer has tried and failed to take over AstraZeneca.

In **biotechnology**, the lead taken by Illumina in sequencing of the human genome has made it the world leader in the field of genetic testing. Its highly sophisticated robots equip laboratories worldwide.

For the **aviation industry**, the advance of Airbus and Boeing gives them assured long-term survival. Orders registered at air shows in 2014 for the new Airbus A330neo give the company hope of 15–20 years of activity for this product. Its development cost €1.5 billion and was entirely self-financed. A similar situation applies to the Boeing 737 MAX.

Other competitive leaderships can also be cited: cheap air travel for Virgin, Ryanair and easyJet; the lithium-ion batteries that give Tesla a decisive lead in the market for electric cars; the new concept of IKEA (democratic design process) that has enabled it to become the world's leading home furnishings company; the new accommodation formula proposed by Airbnb, which has become the world leader in this field, generating turnover of billions of dollars, and which, seven years after its creation, has a market capitalization of $10 billion, exceeding that of the Hyatt group; and the success of Netflix video on demand, which comes from its "vision" of the television of the future—content available on demand on digital media.

Several Belgian examples point in the same direction. Umicore, through innovation, has become a world leader in materials technology. IBA, through its research and innovative products, is the world leader in proton cancer therapy. The same applies to EVS and its system of sport "slow motion". Older examples include the lead given to Solvay for its soda process, the boost given to the Coppée group through its coke ovens, to Bekaert for its steel cords for radial tyres, and to Picanol for its looms. Innovations by Magotteaux gave it 90% of the global market over a long period for their grinding balls. The companies producing billiard balls and cloths (Saluc and Simonis) are world leaders in their niches. Sioen dominates the market for tarpaulins, Puratos that for yeast, Deme, Denul and Vanhool for dredging and marine works, and so many others who, through their creativity, ensure an industrial presence in global markets.

These temporary monopolies and their competitive "advances" do not last very long and tend to decrease over time. New products become more common, imitations appear and supply multiplies, prices fall and income erodes. Three years ago, the Apple iPad was the undisputed leader and largely dominated the market. Today, other brands have developed, reducing Apple to 27% of the global market. Samsung, the world's leading smartphone manufacturer, already considers the golden age of this product to be past. Just eight years after their launch, it is preparing for the "post-smartphone era"[23], while IBM was able to stay ahead in the mainframe computer sector for decades!

We should add that, in becoming great and rich, the most innovative companies tend to become bureaucratic and unable to follow the course of technological progress. Even the most successful are in danger staying in their comfort zone, preferring profit maximization to the risks of new developments. We then see some of them turn into conformist and closed bureaucracies. This can happen to the best of them, at least momentarily. It is interesting to note that IBM, at its zenith, refused to hire Steve Jobs, the future founder of Apple, and missed out on long-term leadership in the PC market (their initial dominance was short-lived). More recently, Facebook rejected a job application from Jan Koum and Brian Acton, co-founders of WhatsApp, the global mobile messaging service that was bought by the same Facebook for

---

23 S. Filipetti, "Samsung, le danger de la succession", *Le Figaro*, 16–17 August 2014.

$19 billion. However, many companies have become sufficiently entrepreneurial to transform over time and to stay active for very long periods.

This collective entrepreneurial approach confirms the true nature of competition and Schumpeter's theory, despite the doubts he may have had at the end of his life. Entrepreneurship really means changing an existing order. The conventional theoretical foundations of our business model describe only very imperfectly its practical operation, and so it can be assumed that Schumpeter's entrepreneurial theory gives a fairly realistic description.

The entrepreneurial chain and corporate culture

Even if innovation has become more systematic, we should not conclude that it has become routine or predictable. It continues to depend on exceptional creative individuals or entrepreneurial businesses acting in an environment used to rupture and change. Innovation is not just a matter of technique or calculation. Like science, it is unpredictable and cannot be fully programmed. It is born of a culture and a mindset that values initiative, momentum and movement. It is a maze of vision, research, energy, intuition, and trial and error. It fluctuates, hesitates, recovers, drives. It cannot be fully codified. It is constantly renewed. It largely escapes analysis, theory and models. This means that the innovation process is fragile.

Individual entrepreneurs may encounter a thousand obstacles in the development of their initiative: the difficulty of finding financing; administrative complexity; resistance to change; difficulty moving beyond the SME stage to internationalize... The capacity of big business to innovate continuously risks being overwhelmed by the size of the stakes, the size of global competitors and the acceleration of the race. It also depends on the economic and social climate of the country where it is located: taxation, social legislation, public policies...

At the scale of a country or group of countries, the development of an adequate business infrastructure and culture to remain competitive is only possible if the environment is sufficiently favourable. It is a complex problem because it affects the mentality and the very culture of society. Entrepreneurship is not decreed but we can encourage the creation of favourable conditions for its emergence.

In a previous generation, President Pompidou asked the Stanford Research Institute to study the conditions for the establishment in France of a "Route 128", the concentration of electronics innovations around

Boston that relied on a dense university network. This wellspring of entrepreneurs and innovation was later followed by Silicon Valley in California, and the city of Seattle. The conclusion of American engineering consultants was that the chances of success in France were very weak because it lacked several key elements of a culture and an ecosystem favourable for entrepreneurs and innovation.[24]

Here we can use the concept of an "**entrepreneurial chain**".[25] The key links in the chain would be: diverse economic fabric; academic openness and density; state of scientific research and collective know-how; clusters of competences; expertise in the sectors of the future; cohabitation of global companies, innovative SMEs and individual entrepreneurs; financing facility; administrative and institutional simplicity; public orders; tolerance of failure; the attitude of the business towards risk and success... If one link is weak, the whole chain is weakened.

It is by developing each of these links that the US has created their famous entrepreneurial culture,

---

24 This pessimism seems to be confirmed by a report of the Economic Analysis Council (2014) that talks of the "vicious circle" that threatens France if it fails to participate sufficiently in the main niches of the future.

25 See P. de Woot, *High Technology Europe: Strategic Issues for Global Competitiveness* (Basil Blackwell, 1990).

thereby developing a real creative process of competitiveness. Their great innovative capacity compared with Europe is as much a culture of risk and tolerance to failure and institutional simplicity as it is one of scientific research, financial resources or public procurement.

Europe, by contrast, in the absence of integration, risks entering into a destructive process of competitiveness. If Europe is strong in its universities and research, it is weak in many other links in the entrepreneurial chain: distrust of business;[26] risk aversion; few large projects; inadequately sized enterprises; scarcity of venture capital; administrative complications… Our leading companies are "national champions" at risk of becoming too small to face global competition. They are not sufficiently present in large niches. We should recall that, with the exception of telecommunications,[27] Europe has almost no global leadership in the information technology and digital communication sector.[28] In space,

26 It was only in 2014 that the dean of the Poitiers Faculty of Social Sciences acknowledged that "business is no longer the devil. There has been a change among professors" (*Le Monde*, 11 September 2014).
27 Threatened today by the significant consolidation of key players.
28 At their zenith (2003), these technologies represented 11.5% of the GDP of the US against 7.5% in the eurozone.

its position is slightly better, but will it be able to save Ariane when faced with the new SpaceX rocket from the American innovator Elon Musk? The recent failure of the launch of two Galileo satellites could make us doubt Europe's ability to carry out very large projects based on the cooperation of states and national "champions". Yet every time that Europe has managed to unify its efforts, it has been able to conquer important global leaderships, for example with Airbus and the Ariane rockets.

At the Treaty of Lisbon in 2007, political leaders pledged to make the European Union, by 2010, "the most competitive knowledge-based economy in the world, capable of sustainable economic growth with quantitative and qualitative employment growth, greater social cohesion, and respect for the environment". It is still far from this! If we are to maintain Europe's economic dynamics, it is imperative that we improve our understanding of the true drivers of development and implement common policies at that level. Affirmative statements do not suffice.

Other examples further illustrate these differences between the US and Europe.

In the area of **shale gas**, the difference in culture is clear. Some European countries even refuse an inventory of their soil, while the Americans set to shale with gusto, found its negative effects and are now trying to correct them. The same analysis applies to **biofuels**: the second-generation bioethanol, using only the stems, leaves and bark, is trying to correct the drawbacks of the former solution, even though results are not yet convincing. Regarding **GMOs**, Europe has shown itself unable to take a position on their use.

Public procurement and industrial policies play an important role in stimulating and developing innovation. In the US, military and space developments have exercised a decisive influence on the creation of new technologies. In Japan, the Ministry of International Trade and Industry (MITI) has long informed the long-term business outlook, clearly defining national goals and industrial policies that support it. This is not the case in Europe. If the European Commission has competition policy in its powers, it cannot take care of industrial policy. Its vision of competition has long hampered business groupings for fear of abuse of power within the common market, while strategic issues were at a global level where the American and Japanese "champions" dominate. As for research and development policy, in the absence of large European budgets, it is more indicative than effective. As economic policy has up to now ignored the actual conditions of competition by innovation, its overly exclusive emphasis on fiscal balance will not only be inefficient but negative. The globalization of competition and technological progress is advancing much faster than European unification. This partly explains the weak presence of major European leaders in new technological fields.

In the US, **venture capital** is abundant. In 2000, US start-ups raised $90 billion from venture capital funds and their success encourages this type of financing. It is also encouraged by the "opt-out" of successful venture capitalists: 59 initial public offerings (IPOs) for the first half of 2014 and 360 acquired companies.[29] In France, SMEs are financed 92% by debt rather than capital, while this ratio is only 50% in the UK and 20% in the US. It is not without reason that the average age of the CAC 40 companies is over a century, while the US continue to rejuvenate their base of "champions".

The size of European companies in the sectors of the future is often insufficient to achieve world leadership. In the US, by contrast, the spread of innovation and availability of venture capital promote rapid growth and occupation of the global market. This is

29 CB Insights, cited by J. Marin, "Investissements record dans les start-up de la Silicon Valley", *Le Monde*, 3–4 August 2014.

where most world champions in new sectors were developed. Three young companies (Apple, Google and Microsoft) are in the top five of world rankings. Of the 100 largest market capitalizations in the world at the time of writing in July 2014, 43 were American companies against 35 in 2008; only 14 were European against 26 in 2008. In the new sectors, innovative performance quickly creates the "giants". The GAFA (Google, Apple, Facebook, and Amazon) are of such a scale that the playing field is completely uneven for latecomers, which is now the position held by Europeans.

The proliferation of "incubators" for start-ups in Europe is an encouraging sign. The major European universities, through their cutting-edge research and science parks, are preparing our economic future in a serious way. They contribute to the creation of a renewed entrepreneurial fabric but, if the other links in the chain are weak, these innovative new branches will struggle to take off and conquer world markets. Many of them will soon be outdated or sold to US multinationals. It is at the European level that any entrepreneurial chain must be strengthened.

Germany has developed its "entrepreneurial chain" better than some countries in southern Europe. Over the past decade, each year its trade balance experienced a surplus of over €100 billion (€190 billion in

2012), while that of France was in deficit throughout the period (–€67 billion in 2012).[30] This difference is explained by innovation and high-end quality. For the automobile sector, for example, this was the choice of Germany while the French were positioned in the middle ranges, much more sensitive to price factors and changes in foreign exchange rates. The respective expenditures in scientific research and technology development reflect and explain this difference. This is the kind of reality that must be kept in mind when dealing with the de-industrialization of Europe. The magnificent success of the great German SMEs is due to innovation. They have managed to create and maintain global leadership positions in narrow high-technology and high-end niches.

The acceleration of innovation is often driven by the appearance of **major new technological branches**. A **branch** can be defined as the set of industry innovations and activities that emerge from a discovery or a major development, such as the steam engine, electricity, the Internet or the human genome. These breakthrough innovations—or meta-technologies—cause further innovation clusters and strongly contribute to the dissemination of technical creativity. They control the evolution of a wide variety of

30 *Sources*: Bloomberg; customs; COF-REXECODE.

sectors and push them to innovate and transform. The Biological Revolution, for example, has only just begun. It will touch many economic sectors as soon as we progress from the discovery of the structure of genes to the development of tools to manipulate them. Its impact will quickly spread to the biomedical, agri-food, materials science and chemistry fields, and others. It is the same for nanotechnology. The convergence of scientific disciplines announces the arrival of major industries and new waves of innovation. This is undoubtedly the case for the coming convergence of biotechnology, nanotechnology and cognitive sciences.

The most obvious current example of disruptive innovation is that of **information and communication technology**. Simplifying greatly, we should reiterate the fact that there have been three major waves: computers, software and networks. Each has spawned countless innovations in equipment (computers, tablets, consoles, smartphones), communication systems and connections (cable, satellite, Internet, search engines, portals...), and applications (social networks, e-commerce ...). At any given time, new platforms, websites and applications are emerging online. Some of them quickly spread worldwide. A list of merely the most visible of them illustrates the creative dynamism engendered by a new branch and the interest for an economy in having major players competing in the same branch such as Netflix, Facebook, Twitter, Yahoo, Wikipedia, eBay, Amazon, WhatsApp, Airbnb, Uber... The next battle will involve the proliferation of connected objects, such as cars, watches and sunglasses, and the integration of application software in equipment.

The **space sector** set in motion thousands of businesses in such diverse and important fields as aerospace, communications, launchers, miniaturized research instruments, navigation and earth observation satellites, physics, chemistry, human foodstuffs, spaceflight, etc. This could also be the case with new energies, nanotechnology and 3D printers (additive manufacturing), which could affect a growing number of sectors, both for manufacturing and for the creation of new products. We should also mention home automation, "the city of the future" (sustainable smart towns) and preventative medicine. It is in these sectors that we will see most future innovations, investment and employment drivers. This is where the development of our economies will come from, and what will contest existing leaderships. These new sectors confirm that innovation is far from disappearing or becoming trivial.

The innovation branches of the future are the subject of many studies and programmes for the European

Commission[31] and governments. But the problem is to encourage enough entrepreneurs to put words into action and to build a strong competitive advantage. It is not only in pricing strategies or evolving costs or in the fiscal balances that our economic future can be read. It is in the creativity of our companies and their ability to establish themselves in these sectors of the future and to conquer global leaderships.

31 The 7th European Union Framework Programme for research focuses on nine sectors: Health; Food, Agriculture and Biotechnology; Information and Communications Technology; Nanosciences, Nanotechnologies, Materials and new Production Technologies; Energy; Environment (including climate change); Transport (including aeronautics); Socio-economic Sciences and Humanities; Security and Space.

2

Innovation, fairness and the common good

We have seen how this type of competition by innovation is powerful and how the necessity to constantly race ahead is constraining. It is time now to discuss this type of development from the point of view of society and social fairness. The destructive aspect of an economic system based on permanent innovation may be very high for society: it may cause social stress and great human suffering. Then new applications of science and technology are becoming more ambiguous, especially if we consider the opportunities opened by the convergence of nanotechnologies, biosciences and artificial intelligence. And, last but not least, the management of this destructive creativity is mostly left in private hands. The enterprises are the key decision-takers in a system led by a logic of means—its own development—and not by a logic of ends and values.

Woe to the vanquished: creative destruction

If development through innovation is discontinuous, random and risky, it is also **brutal and dangerous**.[32] In the short term, it can be economically and socially costly. We are in a Darwinian world where only the fittest survive.

Industrial and commercial structures are constantly challenged, and losers disappear or are bought out.

If the company loses its leadership position, misses the necessary technological shift or has no relay products, the cost is high. A delay in innovation causes a loss of competitiveness resulting in plant closures, mass lay-offs and sometimes local desertification. This brutality is illustrated by the collapse of many newer leaders who have ceased to innovate or have not been fast enough: Nokia, Blackberry, Oracle, Dell, Motorola... Older cases are legion: Kodak, Creusot-Loire, ACEC, Vieille Montagne, Cockerill, Olivetti,

32 Lisbon Group, *Limits to Competition* (Cambridge, MA: MIT Press, 1995).

General Motors, the Empain group, Société Générale de Belgique...

In 2007, Nokia, with 40% of the world market, was the undisputed leader in mobile telephony. This was the year of Apple's smartphone launch. Nokia had no faith in it and missed this strategic shift. Six years later, its mobile phone division was bought by Microsoft, losing in the process half of its jobs worldwide. Finland felt betrayed and the prime minister gave a good description of the destructive side of competition: "We rested on two pillars: one was high technologies with Nokia, another the paper industry. The iPhone has damaged Nokia, and the iPad the wood industry."[33] In the same field, Blackberry, the smartphone pioneer overtaken by Apple and Samsung, laid off 40% of its workforce. It was worth $100 billion in 2007 but it was worth less than $5 billion at the time of writing in July 2014. It's the same for Sony, which has carried out successive waves of lay-offs in the mobile telephony sector.

Other examples can be cited. Half of independent bookstores are threatened by Amazon and e-commerce. Urban taxis are facing a full-frontal attack by Uber and its app offering cars with drivers. The press lives under the sword of Damocles because of the

33 The iPad reduces the need for paper pulp.

Internet and new connectivity; it will survive only by converting to digital. The publishers of the major encyclopaedias (such as *Encyclopaedia Universalis* and *Encyclopaedia Britannica*) are severely threatened by Wikipedia. It is the same for television, which is violently challenged by Internet giants eager to seize its advertising dollars. Netflix, the US streaming champion, threatens to disrupt the structure of the audio-visual industry. With contactless payment (Apple Pay), Apple becomes a threat of disintermediation for all existing players such as banks and even PayPal.[34] The desktop PC sector is in danger from the tidal wave of smartphones that are beginning to dominate Internet traffic. More than half of airlines are directly threatened by low-cost competition. Every day the media announces brutal attacks: it talks about hold-ups in a particular sector, revolutions, obsolescence, carnage.

Entire sectors disappear when their competitiveness decreases owing to the loss of technical leadership or of a cost advantage. In a globalized economy, reorganizations, takeovers and mergers, to reach a global scale, are becoming more frequent. This is the change that Schumpeter called "control of larger

---

34 "Apple Pay will change forever the way we buy things" (Tim Cook, CEO of Apple).

units". This type of change can be very brutal too. In the steel industry, for example, the absorption of European companies by ArcelorMittal has caused plant closures and major lay-offs. It is the same for the automotive industry or sectors that are relocating to countries with low costs. One of the few weapons against such threats is to keep a technological edge, as does Germany.

This **rate of change** applies to the whole society that is struggling to adapt to the accelerating speed of technological progress.

We have entered a race whose speed is dictated by business dynamism and competitive games. The brutal accelerator role played by technological competition continues to grow and become widespread. The new constantly replaces the old; the past is rapidly replaced by the future. This incessant race means an almost permanent change in culture. "Those who benefit the first from these major changes are primarily those who received good training. Hence the emergence of new inequalities: woe to non-graduates when the world changes!"[35] In the digital sector, it is clear that job creation penalizes the least skilled.

This rhythm is much faster than the adaptive capacity of political, civil or institutional society. Our

---

35 L. Ferry, *L'innovation destructice* (Paris: Plon, 2014).

administrative, educational and social systems adapt with more and more difficulty. This divergence creates a growing threat of inequality, exclusion, unemployment, precariousness and social breakdown. We start to run the risk of the system crushing people. If the logic of economic and technical innovation is that of creative destruction, one wonders whether today, for some categories of people, the destructive effects of creation do not outweigh its benefits. In other words, is the human cost of such rapid change not too high?

Our economic system is not only one of creative dynamism, growth and progress, it is also marked by instability, crises and social suffering. The recent crisis has caused a resurgence of insecurity in most European countries without the indebted public authorities, under the control of financial markets and the stress of "competitiveness", seeming to really be able to help. This uncertainty can be such that life becomes unbearable. Can one live life to the best when one is unable to direct it? This increases social division and loss of confidence in the existing model. This also increases distress and suffering, as is particularly indicated by the growing number of suicides at work.

More profoundly, an existential approach[36] to this system shows that our business model can also be a force for alienation, an absurd dynamic in which the true meaning of existence is lost. The productivist obsession, competitive forward flight, loss of independence, loss of collective values "leads us to think with Rimbaud that real life is elsewhere." "Why is it that our businesses, whose creative activity should justify, are so often destructive to humanity?"[37]

Prometheus or the ambiguity of economic and technical creativity

The incredible series of innovations in the Neolithic period is initially seen in terms of progress for humanity. But there is another side to such technical creation: the fear of consequences and the question about the limits and dangers of unbridled use of new tools. This concern raises questions about the meaning of this creativity.

In Greek mythology, innovators and creators of material progress are heroes, titans and gods, but

36 C. Arnsperger, *Critique de l'existence capitaliste* (Paris: Cerf, 2005).
37 X. Grenet, *Cahiers d'un DRH* (Paris: Cerf, 2008).

they are also cursed: Prometheus is chained; Ulysses cannot go home; Jason loses his children killed by Medea; Hercules is burned in the shirt of Nessus; Icarus crashes; and Vulcan is lame and deceived.[38] Why are they cursed? Over the centuries, this question is close to our current interrogations.

By chaining Prometheus, Aeschylus questions us about the ambiguity of a non-finalized creativity and unlimited entrepreneurial power. For the masters of technical creation, the temptation of excess, of hubris, is constantly present. Prometheus was struck by it. The gods then chained him to a rock where, every morning, an eagle gnawed on his liver. The dialogue that follows speaks of the ambivalence of technical progress without values.

My name is clairvoyant, I who knows, Prometheus the subtle... deliverer of men... I healed humans from the terrors of death. And when the chorus of Oceanides, astonished by this extraordinary statement, asked: *but what remedy did you find for them?* Prometheus answers: *a blindfold, blind hope.*

Blindness! Refusal to question the meaning of technical progress.

---

38 See P. de Woot, *Should Prometheus Be Bound?* (Palgrave Macmillan, 2005).

A Chinese myth also speaks of the concern raised by masters of technical creativity. In ancient times, blacksmiths became kings when they made the largest and most beautiful bronze vase. After ten years, they had to produce another that surpassed the first one in beauty. In order for the vessel to be perfect, they had to throw themselves in the furnace with their wives. The Chinese thus limited the power of these demiurges they considered dangerous. They admired the masters of the art, but they also feared their power. The myth says that kings soon realized that the wives alone would be enough to make the perfect vessel, and they thus retained life and power.[39]

Faced with scientific and technical advances, George Steiner, in his essay on culture, poses the same question.[40] Unlike art, he says, science works by accumulation and development becomes exponential. This gradually escapes the realm of democratic debate. By their magnitude and acceleration, science and technology have gained momentum and autonomy that may lead them onto dangerous paths. "Any definition of later classical civilization must learn to take into account scientific knowledge and

39 M. Granet, *La civilisation chinoise*, l'Évolution de l'Humanité (Albin Michel, 1968).
40 G. Steiner, *Dans le château de Barbe Bleue. Note pour une redéfinition de la culture* (Paris: Seuil, 1973).

the world of mathematics and symbolic languages. For they alone hold omnipotence: in fact as well as in the fever of progress that defines us..."

Einstein raised the same question when he said: "We must acknowledge that there is no path that leads from the knowledge of what *is* to what *needs to be*".[41]

Isabelle Stengers takes up this theme and suggests that science should agree to question its purpose and role in society. The application of science and technical guidance is obviously not neutral.

The philosopher Jean-Pierre Dupuy warns of unprecedented new opportunities looming on the horizon:

> With the convergence of nanotechnology and biotechnology, man takes over biological processes. He participates in the production of life. However, the one who wants to make life cannot aim to replicate its essential capacity, which is in its turn to create something radically new. His ambition being to ultimately trigger irreversible processes in nature, the engineer of tomorrow will not be a sorcerer's apprentice by negligence or incompetence, but by design. It's fascinating and scary at the same time.[42]

41 A. Einstein, *Selected Works* (Le Seuil/CNRS, 1991, Vol. 5).
42 J.P. Dupuy, "Le progrès technique pour quoi faire?", *Le Monde*, 12 November 2014; see also *L'Avenir de l'économie.*

Europe, however, finds it more and more difficult to objectively answer questions posed by the advance of science. It is torn between the "merchants of doubt" and the "merchants of fear" of civil society.[43]

The use made of it can sometimes make the innovation seem harmful and threatening. This is what makes the precautionary principle a necessary ethical approach for any entrepreneur who wants to be responsible.

> With his ingenious knowledge, which exceeds all expectations, man progresses toward good or evil? (Sophocles)

A few examples will suffice to illustrate this point.

Biogenetics promises abundant harvests, the healing of incurable diseases and the extending of our lives without too much decay. But it also raises the spectre of genetic manipulation with unpredictable consequences, affecting the nature of humans and all living species.

Sortir de l'éco mystification (Flammarion, 2012) and *Pour un catastrophisme éclairé: quand l'impossible est certain* (Seuil, 2004).

43 See N. Oreskès and E.M. Conway, *Merchants of Doubt* (Bloomsbury Press, 2010); see also S. Delpont, "Sortons des controverses sur l'innovation", *Le Monde*, 24 September, 2014.

Nanotechnologies announce countless innovations in the most varied fields but, without regulation, they might pose serious health and environmental problems.

Nuclear science screens for diseases, heals some cancers and can protect food, mail and medical instruments from any contamination. It provides energy that does not pollute the atmosphere, but the long-term disposal of its waste is a threat. It can become a formidable instrument of deterrence in the hands of the rulers and the military, but also of blackmail and terror in the hands of extremists or "rogue states". Humans now face the possibility of destroying their own kind.

The **Internet** opens up new vistas of information, interactive communication, exchange, debate and education. It could create the neo-sphere dear to Teilhard de Chardin and facilitate the advent of a world united in its diversity. But it also carries with it all possible aspects of a world subject to information overload, simplifications, ratings, and confinement to narrow specializations or identity fantasies. It can also boost global security threats, mafia networks and ad nauseam broadcasting of images of violence. It also requires us to completely rethink some basic concepts such as the protection of privacy that hyper-connectivity, geo-location and the marketing of personal data already do not respect. Cyber monitoring conducted by American services clearly shows the ambivalence of this technological advance. Big Brother is close to Big Data. On another level, the massive exploitation of existing information on the Internet (cloud computing) actually risks decreasing our analytical capabilities by flooding us with correlated data that does not in fact link cause and effect.[44]

Financial innovations have undoubtedly made the market more fluid but we know the damage they have created by the low intelligibility of their new products, their indiscriminate use and their inherent limitations. So much so that one comedian has said that the only useful financial innovation for the customer is the ATM.

Shale oil and gas are now the dominant innovations in the energy field. Ambiguity is evident. It allows the US to have abundant energy and low prices, to regain its independence in this area and to initiate re-industrialization, growth and job creation processes. But, at the same time, current operating methods have a real risk of polluting water and the atmosphere. We noted earlier the different reactions of Europe and the US when faced with this ambivalence.

---

44 According to Disraeli, there are three types of lies: lies, damned lies and statistics.

Pesticides (insecticides, fungicides, herbicides, etc.) improve agricultural yields but, beyond some rarely respected risk thresholds, they endanger food security and the health of the workers who handle them.

The ambiguity of technological innovations has created in the public a widespread fear and often excessive distrust of potential progress. Everything related to food, health, the environment and safety is marked by anxiety and lack of objective information. The weaknesses of public expertise, incompetent politicians, superficial presentations by most media and strategies of doubt and misinformation conducted by some companies make it difficult to hold any serious debate on a reasonable application of the famous precautionary principle. The difficulty of anticipating future applications of scientific discovery reinforces people's concern. As Paul Valéry said: "The man often knows what he is doing, but he never knows the results of his actions." We should be aware of the dangers of an unbridled Promethean system that finds its legitimacy in its sole technical superiority, tempted by the "unlimited", and whose delusional optimism make one believe one can try everything, do everything and decide alone upon the application of this Promethean power over science and technology.

There is also that which Luc Ferry called "innovation for innovation"—an innovation that aims only to make the competitor go out of fashion by superficial changes unrelated to true progress.[45] As part of the strategies of "change for change" without direction or purpose, this type of false innovation unnecessarily increases pressure on the company and creates worker insecurity. Planned obsolescence for purely commercial reasons and supported only by compelling advertising cannot be categorized as innovative progress.[46]

Power over the future in an ethical and political vacuum

We have seen that companies have considerable power to act and to direct our development process. They master and use most of the key resources of economic creativity. For many of them, this power is growing globally. Today, the most dynamic and powerful global players are businesses. In fact, they are among the only organizations that have managed

---

45 L. Ferry, 2014, op. cit.

46 Vance Packard had already covered this topic in a famous book *The Hidden Persuaders* (David McKay Co, 1957).

to simultaneously cross all globalization thresholds: size, time horizon, complexity, resources, information and networks. Through their competitive strength, companies have adapted to globalization faster than most of our political, social, legal and educational institutions...[47] This puts them in a strong position for the conquest of resources, strategic choices, direction and pace of growth. They thus have real power over the development of countries and regions, which clearly raises the question of their societal responsibilities.

As we noted above, a key element of this power is the mastery of science and technology. Companies have become major players in the use of scientific knowledge. They are the ones that determine its applications and orientations. The delay in adapting our institutional and political structures may make the orientation of science and technology relevant only to the market rather than directing them at priority, but not necessarily profitable or insolvent, needs. What must be emphasized at this stage is the danger that we run if we delay integrating scientific and technical creativity into a more responsible view

47 The concentration and power of multimedia groups became such that the boss of Time Warner said that they were "more powerful than governments, NGOs and teaching establishments".

of our global future and if we abandon techno-science to its own dynamics and competitive logic. If techno-science is only exposed to a free economic system, it is possible that the **Brave New World** will become a fairy tale.[48] This is especially the case for the applications of scientific discoveries and we should not confuse basic research (the free pursuit of truth) and its transformation into utility.[49]

More generally, this growing power is subject to all the temptations of domination and abuse that usually accompany uncontrolled power. This particularly affects the rules of competition, barriers to entry, the abuse of economic power, cartels, tax evasion, pressures on public authorities, breach of privacy, data security, etc. Recently, abuses have multiplied: manipulation of accounts, debt concealment, tax evasion, insider trading, toxic products, corruption, breach of trust, irresponsible financial lending... Some did not hesitate to cheat, lie, manipulate interbank rates... to the point of being called "banksters" and "cesspool banks".

Today, Amazon, the online distribution giant, is accused of abusing its dominant position to force

---

48 See on this subject: G. Steiner, *Dans le château de Barbe Bleue* (Seuil, 1973).
49 D. Lambert, *Sciences et théologie* (Lessius, 1999).

publishers to lower prices for books sold online, and of manipulating sales to intimidate them. The dominant position of Google worries European players. As it holds 90% of the online search market in Europe, its users and its competitors accuse it of being a monopoly, manipulating search results to promote its own services and degrade those of its competitors. The German boss of media group Axel Springer accuses Google of being a monopoly without transparency or respect for competition. In France, the culture minister rages his impotent wrath in vain. In a globalized economy, is it still realistic to defend a "cultural and digital strategy for France"?

As the company is the agent of choice for economic and technical creativity, it has long been believed that its actions *automatically* serve the common good through the virtues of the market and its famous "invisible hand". Today, this belief is clearly in question. Globalization, the acceleration of techno-science and the lack of global regulation give the economic system unprecedented *autonomy* and power of action. It operates according to its own criteria: profitability, competitiveness and competition for market share. In the absence of global regulation, the instrumental logic tends to become dominant and impose a development model that has no purpose other than its own effectiveness. Its "simplicity" is incompatible with the complexity of a globalized world.

At a global level, companies operate in a **political vacuum**. Economic globalization is advancing much faster than global governance and the necessary regulations. It is beyond the control of the nation states and it gradually imposes its logic on the whole planet. Although economic issues are sometimes over-regulated at the state or European level, they are totally under-regulated globally because of a lack of global governance. This failure by politics to keep up with economics leads to a sort of public powerlessness to drive real development strategies and democratically debate the societal challenges of globalization. As Raymond Aron[50] said, nation states have become too small for the big problems and too big for the small ones. The weakening of states is clearly shown in their failure to address the real challenges of the 21st century, such as global warming, destruction of biodiversity and rising inequality. As discussed below, the weakness of states becomes clear when we look at the desire of industrial or financial lobbies to impose their own standards of conduct or their own scientific expertise in areas such as health and the environment, where risks are difficult to assess.

50 R. Aron, *Paix et guerre entre les nations* (Calmann-Lévy, 1962).

The recent closures by multinational companies of some European industrial sites illustrate this failure of states in respect of global strategies that are developed and executed outside of them. In the case of ArcelorMittal, for example, the French and Belgian governments are almost completely powerless. Although strategies are needed for enterprise, this is a serious problem when it is seen to undermine social cohesion and confidence in a political system. In 2012, Fukuyama[51] reiterated that there is no democracy without the balanced co-existence of a strong state, the rule of law and government accountability. For this author, the decline of civilizations is often explained by the growing strength of interest groups that are beyond political action and can become corrupt. This is what happens when institutions are no longer adapted to reality.

Economic action also takes place in an **ethical vacuum**. Our model operates according to a logic of means and not ends: it aims to maximize the use of scarce resources and the benefits resulting therefrom. It is based on technical, managerial and financial modernity and not on values. This system is amoral. It does not contain in itself any indication other than

---

51 F. Fukuyama, *Le début de l'histoire. Des origines de la politique à nos jours* (Saint Simon, 2012).

that of solvent markets. Without an ethical framework or policy at a global level, it is guided by its instrumental logic.

Beneath the respectable clothing of dynamism and efficiency of open world trade, neoliberal globalization hides a radical ideology, a one-track thought. It is, put simply, too absolute a belief in market efficiency as well as an almost visceral distrust of government intervention and regulation of international economic issues. This approach is overly optimistic. Its faith in the "wisdom" of the markets, the virtue of techno-science and structural adaptability, allows it to ignore competitive inequality, technology ambiguity, the cynicism of the players, and the social costs of restructuring and de-structuring. The believers of this "faith" are, like Pangloss, declaring with a false naivety that everything will be for the best in the best of worlds. And yet, how delusional to think that the market economy is a self-regulating process that automatically contributes to the common good! This approach is based on a truncated view of the role of the enterprise and of its power. Milton Friedman[52] claimed that *the only social responsibility of business*

---

52 M. Friedman, "The Social Responsibility of Business is to Increase its Profits", published in *The New York Times Magazine* on 13 September 1970, and reproduced by practically all business schools.

is the enrichment of the shareholder. This vision, we see every day, leads economic players to adopt unreasonable behaviour whereas economic theory presents them as rational beings. In a globalized neo-liberal model, "we can make a lot of money by being irresponsible; incentives for bad behaviour remain the strongest".[53]

Economic power disconnected from ethics and politics raises two fundamental questions for economic theory: that of power and that of meaning.[54] It is not neoclassical theory or econometrics that has the answer. We must return to the political economy that, in its beginnings, was a moral science. What blindness to believe that the market alone will oversee and direct the power that controls key resources for our future!

53 H. Mintzberg, "Rebuilding Companies as Communities", *Harvard Business Review*, 2009.

54 See P. de Woot, 2005, op. cit. and P. de Woot, *Repenser l'entreprise* (Académie en Poche, 2013); see also L. Ferry, 2014, op. cit.

3
Responsible innovation

To face the challenges of our time, we need innovation like we need bread and we must create the proper climate and culture to develop strong entrepreneurial drive. But, more than ever, we must give this entrepreneurial drive its ethical and societal dimensions. Responsible innovation means a more voluntary orientation towards the great problems of the 21st century: the planet, rising inequalities, new scientific development potentially threatening freedom, democracy and human integrity. We need to transform our increasing creativity into real progress for mankind. In this respect, the rapid development of social innovations opens new ways and practices.

The entrepreneurial imperative

Innovation and creativity are essential to the dynamism of an economy. Faced with the growth of emerging countries, the competitiveness of developed countries mainly depends on innovation.

It is the individual or collective entrepreneurs that give strength to the economy. With their creativity, they take initiatives and make the transformations necessary to survive in a competitive global system. The vitality of the economy depends on a sufficiently active and dense entrepreneurial culture.

If society is ill-suited to the pace of economic and technical creativity, it's not a reason to blame innovation, as Luc Ferry tends to do in his recent book.[55] If one criticism should be made of the market economy, it is not found in human creativity but in the inadequacy of our structures. The creative capacity of humanity is a scarce resource to be cultivated and better focused. We need entrepreneurs and their creativity. Through their innovations, they are able to help us cope with the societal challenges of the 21st century.

This approach is more realistic today, where creativity, innovation and entrepreneurial activity fall outside the sole framework of a capitalist enterprise. Thousands of initiatives appear throughout the world claiming to offer solutions: social entrepreneurship, social economy, fair trade, positive economy... They are a sign of an increased number of entrepreneurial

55 L. Ferry, 2014, op. cit.

and accountable actions. Many of them cooperate with capitalist enterprises that are inspired to transform their culture and fulfil their social responsibilities. This abundance of creativity develops new forms of businesses that, far from competing with more conventional firms, are an indispensable complement and a source of cultural inspiration.

As long as economic theory gives so little importance to innovation and the societal changes it causes, it will continue to produce superficial analyses and ignore the real role of companies, their power and their responsibilities. More importantly, it will be unable to offer the development strategies that are needed much more than mere economic stimulus policies or restrictive measures to balance the budget. It will remain powerless to ask the real ethical questions about our future.

It is at a European scale that the entrepreneurial imperative arises. If one wants to develop a favourable climate for innovation and an entrepreneurial fabric able to conquer global markets, one must exit the classical economic paradigm. Action should be taken in all the links of the entrepreneurial "chain", not only nationally but on an international scale, for example the European Union: new technological sectors, major projects, public orders, advanced research, proliferation of start-ups, plenty of venture

capital, taxation, strategic combinations and crea-
tions of European champions...[56]

Turning creativity into progress

We have seen that corporate power, especially power
over science and technology, is ambiguous. Cut off
from its social purpose, it can become threatening.[57]
To believe, as some economic theory does, that the
market will fix this is an illusion. The market cannot
do everything, and if economic action and thought
lack ethical and political dimensions, the Holy Grail
of economic fairness sought by Jean Pierre Hansen
will not be found.[58] The economy must become again
a moral science. Is it not the societal responsibility of
the entrepreneur to complete his work and to serve
the common good?

56 Recently, major European transport projects (15,000 km of
    high speed line), banking union and the extension of pro-
    ject bonds providing the European Investment Bank (EIB)
    guarantee for the financing of private or public projects are
    moving in the right direction.
57 J. Van Rijckevorsel, *L'entreprise, un moteur de progrès?*
    (Thélès, 2012).
58 See J.P. Hansen, *Une quête de Graal* (Académie
    en Poche, 2014).

Questioning the purpose of entrepreneurial creativity is to question material progress, its focus and its ambiguities. If entrepreneurs want their extraordinary *creativity* to turn into *progress* for humanity, they have a duty to direct, to give it meaning through its moral and societal dimensions. The definition of progress is inseparable from an ethical and political reflection.

Is economic progress not a more serious basis than profit alone to specify the action of entrepreneurs? A more serious basis than quantitative growth alone? A growing number of economists[59] question the concept of growth and its measurement, gross domestic product (GDP). They suggest more refined economic goals, such as sustainable development, "different" growth, prosperity without growth, the green economy, social solidarity... They also have to use other criteria, and other performance measures such as the human development index plus many indicators:

59 See I. Cassiers et al., *Redéfinir la prospérité. Jalons pour un débat public* (L'Aube, 2011); T. Jackson, *Prospérité sans croissance* (De Boeck/Etopia, 2010). See also works on growth and "happiness", particularly B. Frey and A. Stutzer, *Happiness and Economics* (Princeton University Press, 2002); see also See also R. Gaucher, *Bonheur et économie* (L'Harmattan, 2009) and R. Layard, G. Mayraz and S.J. Nickell, *The Marginal Utility of Income* (London School of Economics and Political Science, 2007).

ecological footprint, "living better", "real progress", "national happiness", etc.

To give a responsible meaning to entrepreneurial action, one has to reflect on and answer the following questions:

Economic and technical creativity
- Why?
- For whom?
- How?

The answers to these questions can only be ethical and political. The market alone is unable to respond.

- *Why?* Is it really necessary that our economic empowerment and our extraordinary creative ability should be devoted exclusively to developing only solvent markets and the unceasing hyper-consumption of a society driven by feverish and pervasive advertising? Are there no other priorities in the world that are not being met and whose importance is incommensurate with advanced hyper-comfort or leisure pursuits?

- *For whom?* Is it morally acceptable and politically reasonable to tolerate the fact that half of humanity is still excluded from the benefits of the creativity and dynamism of an economy that works without it or against it? How long will we tolerate the paradox of creating wealth unparalleled in human history and such an unjust distribution of that wealth?

- *How?* Will the creativity of business prioritize the race for growth to which rich countries are committed? Will this race continue to pollute the atmosphere, destroy its limited resources and foster a kind of individualistic and selfish society, trapped in the bubble of its success and privileges? Would the capacity to innovate not be better directed towards the priority problems of the planet and humanity?

Entrepreneurs cannot answer those questions alone. They will be increasingly drawn to political debate and ethical reflection. We should recall that the European tradition from Aristotle considers economics, ethics and politics to be part of the same set.[60] This is a significant cultural shift that goes further than most discourse on social responsibilities. It is all the more necessary given that we are faced with challenges that go beyond our policy and institutional frameworks: population growth, pockets of extreme poverty, inequalities in education, health

60 European Commission, *Livre Blanc sur la Gouvernance* (Brussels, 2001).

and employment, crisis and social anxiety, migration, violence and radicalization, climate change, destruction of biodiversity, ocean pollution, and the dichotomy between political governance and the global economy.

Embedding a social imperative in entrepreneurial action means integrating creativity within the context of wider challenges and sustainable development. We must stop pretending that there is an automatic convergence of the current economic creativity and overall development of humanity. We must stop claiming that only personal interest must guide economic behaviour and respond to global challenges; simply trusting in technical ingenuity and market indications is misguided. Choices are necessary. A company will only be responsible if it operates with a view to human and sustainable development.

From this perspective, we propose defining the purpose of the company as follows: **the creation of economic and societal progress in a sustainable and globally responsible manner.**[61]

Economic progress is only a subset; it should not dominate society to impose its limited vision of progress. Other forms of progress exist in cultural, social,

---

61 Globally Responsible Leadership Initiative (GRLI), *A Call to Action* (Brussels, 2005).

political, spiritual, and educational realms. While economic progress promotes some of them, it does not cover the whole field of human progress.

But economic progress is created by the innovative companies. They have created it through ruptures, destruction and drift, but we must recognize that they are the source of continuous material progress for people and societies who can benefit from their creativity.

In human history, what greater odyssey than this progress?

Marx himself was amazed by our creativity: "The bourgeoisie ... has accomplished wonders far surpassing Egyptian pyramids, Roman aqueducts, and Gothic cathedrals"[62] He added: "it has conducted expeditions that put in the shade all former Exoduses of nations and crusades."

On the death of Steve Jobs, Apple's creator, the global press celebrated his exceptional merits. "The world has lost a visionary and creative genius." More recently, the French "boss of bosses", Pierre Gattaz, concerned about the lack of economic audacity on the part of the French government,

---

62 K. Marx, *Manifesto of the Communist Party* (1848), available at: www.marxists.org/archive/marx/works/1848/communist-manifesto/ch01.htm.

exclaimed: "Entrepreneurs are heroes and we must tell them that!" An echo of the Greek mythology mentioned above!

Despite the failures and deviations of the market economy,[63] it is the individual and collective entrepreneurs who, in the wake of science, are behind the concrete improvements in the lives of hundreds of millions of people: housing, health, transport, information, communication and entertainment. In the long term, it is through creativity that companies provide material progress, but also employment and the competitiveness of regions, countries and continents. This is also where the keys to economic development lie.

A more societal focus of creative capacity

A company that wants to be responsible can contribute with others to solving the global problems of the 21st century and correcting major dysfunctions of our business model.

Entrepreneurship, creativity and innovation are necessary answers to the challenges of our time. As for the current excesses of a market economy led by

---

63 P. de Woot, *Repenser l'entreprise* (Académie en Poche, 2013).

instrumental logic, the enterprise, rather than contributing to the problem, may become the *solution*. It is here that it will find its true social responsibility.

It is important to rethink the direction of its creative power and its development strategies. In many sectors, companies have already begun to do so.

The environment and saving the planet are now major challenges. Many companies are beginning to deal with this by directing their creative capacity towards innovative solutions. One must not overestimate the ability of companies to come up with a sustainable business model. The pressures of the markets are often stronger than the will of leaders to become more responsible. Nevertheless, the movement towards socially responsible business is growing. In the face of global challenges, new solutions continue to be invented and implemented. And it is the collective or individual entrepreneurs who are doing this.

Many companies are starting to get into a pattern of a "circular economy" to reduce their environmental footprint. Several major industries such as automotive, aviation, construction and energy are launching research and innovating in the very design of products to make them more environmentally friendly. Other sectors are inaugurating a "service economy" that focuses on use rather than ownership. This is particularly the case with Michelin, which began selling distances instead of tyres. This is also the case of the "sharing economy" in the fields of transport, holidays and household equipment. In the US, it is the leaders of some multinational companies such as Coca-Cola and Nike that are seeking to stir an indifferent public and sound the environmental alarm.

Let us pause for a moment on an exemplary case of **recycling**: Umicore, the Belgian rare metals and new materials company that has decided to reinvent and transform its core business. From the high-polluting activity of mining and refining metals, it has become a high-tech company in the field of recovery and processing of rare metals as well as in new materials. It has opted for a culture of sustainable development and yet is pitched at a high level of performance and profitability.

Poverty and inequality are beginning to influence the strategies of some companies. They have adopted the perspective of Amartya Sen, who suggests guiding the company's creative capacity more towards the "bottom of the pyramid". The intention is that through innovation they are able to meet less creditworthy or non-solvent needs. Entrepreneurial creativity can help address extreme poverty. In attempting to make entrepreneurs, it can also initiate a genuine dynamic development. Some examples are already visible and persuasive: the Grameen Bank and microcredit, the Transformational Business Network, Danone Communities, Essilor and Aravind in India, the Shell Foundation, Lafarge South Africa, the Bill and Melinda Gates Foundation… Some researchers are working on a new and strong hypothesis: companies that voluntarily confront poverty, fragility, the disabled and the marginalized can themselves be transformed and deeply change their purpose, mindset and culture.

An interesting example is that of **Essilor**, the world leader in ophthalmic lenses. Its entrepreneurial strategy is based on two pillars: science and technology leadership and global commercial leadership. This is a classic approach and led the company to high economic and financial performance. In India, Essilor placed its technological capacity in the service of the poor. In partnership with an Indian hospital group, Aravind, it takes care of those at the "bottom of the pyramid". Aravind has for 20 years provided the poorest Indian people with free cataract operations. Essilor has set up laboratories in field hospitals for eye tests and the manufacture of corrective lenses. Through this approach, it was able to adapt its technology to suit the production cost of Indian campaigns. There is no question here of philanthropy but of a core technological capacity steered to help the poorest.

Danone is also a good example of this new corporate responsibility. The company has created a foundation to promote the emergence of young entrepreneurs in the poorest regions: Danone Communities. Its mission is to provide finance and to develop, with the expertise and technology of Danone, local businesses with a sustainable economic model that is oriented towards social goals: reducing poverty and malnutrition. On the part of social entrepreneurs, this support involves both investment via public mutual funds and technical support through a network of committed experts who transmit their experience. The Danone Communities partnership with the Grameen Bank and Ashoka for social incubators is an interesting extension of this focus. Beyond its projects, Danone wants to share its teachings to inspire other individual and collective initiatives in the service of a more cohesive society.

Some high-tech companies, confident in their ability to innovate, have clearly announced their intention to serve the common good. Champions of the Internet are beginning to put their skills at the service of great social causes such as health, research, education and knowledge. Several examples can be used to illustrate this approach.

Google is expanding its ambitions by entering the field of health. It presents itself, 15 years after its creation, as a "grand enterprise of human progress". It highlights projects such as Calico, the start-up dedicated to the extension of human life. It is also striving to draw the molecular portrait of a healthy body in association with Stanford University and Duke University. The genetic and molecular library allows early detection of health disparities and improves preventative medicine. An alliance with Novartis will also allow it to create intelligent lenses for presbyopia and diabetes (for blood sugar control). An innovative start-up acquisition strategy further broadens their leadership.

Facebook is leading a project that brings together seven Internet giants to make the Web accessible anywhere in the world. This project aims to reduce the cost of Internet access and also to develop new approaches to connect the five billion people who are not connected. Under the slogan "connect the next billion people", Facebook has already invested a billion dollars to connect people in developing countries.

The ten largest pharmaceutical companies in the world (Big Pharma) have joined forces to develop new treatments against Alzheimer's disease, diabetes and arthritis. They will share their data and researchers.[64]

64 C. Hecketsweiler, "Les géants de la pharmacie unissent leurs forces", *Le Monde*, 6 February 2014.

The French start-up Pixium is preparing to market a high-tech implant able to "give sight" to the blind through signals transmitted by the optic nerve to the brain that decodes them to form images in black and white.[65]

New technologies such as "Big Data", the "Cloud" and connected objects are being used to guide further health systems towards a better understanding of disease and treatment and towards preventative and personalized medicine.[66]

Even **more traditional areas** can turn problems into solutions. The coal sector, for example, is developing new technologies that dramatically reduce emissions of greenhouse gases. Through innovative techniques for the capture and storage of CO_2, Sakspower in Canada is, for the first time, producing coal without emitting pollutant gases. This is a major prospect for countries such as China and Poland whose basic energy is coal.

Access to clean toilets determines the health of part of the world population. Again, it is innovations that provide solutions. These are multiplying today, under the impetus of the Bill and Melinda Gates

65　Idem, "Pixium redonne la vue aux aveugles", *Le Monde*, 3 May 2014.

66　See Renaissance Numérique, *Livre blanc. D'un modèle de santé curatif à un modèle de santé curatif* (Paris, 2014).

Foundation. "Future toilets" is a very active area of research and innovation. Technical progress will contribute in a major way to meet the challenges of the 21st century. However, we must not believe that this will suffice. The pressure of nine billion people and the physical limits of the planet will also force us to change our behaviour and our social rules.[67]

Ethics, politics and the techno-sciences[68]

Science cannot be shielded from ethics. Today, science is tightly bound to technology and poses most unusual questions in matters of ethics, beginning with its own status. While the independence of science and its freedom of approach are the reasons for its excellence, the use of its results and the orientation of its research step into the field of ethics and politics.[69] There are several reasons for this.

The first is the ambiguity of its applications. Science has always been a source of optimism and wonder for mankind but also of concerns and fears. The myth of Prometheus clearly alludes to this, as

67 P. Bihouix, *L'âge des low tech* (Seuil, 2014).
68 See P. de Woot, 2005, op. cit.
69 D. Lambert, *Science et théologie* (Lessius, 1999).

does the story of the tree of knowledge in the Bible. Sophocles also referred to this ambiguity: "with his ingenious knowledge which exceeds all expectation man progresses toward evil or toward good".[70]

The second reason is its proliferation and acceleration, which are outstripping the understanding of people and the pace of social debate

A third reason why science should be subject to ethics is its increasingly close union with technology. Firms have turned it into a competitive weapon. The time between research and concrete application is ever shorter and there is less and less public debate. It is economic and financial criteria that determine the transformation of scientific discoveries into commercial truths. This confers on the techno-sciences an immense power to influence the evolution of human society. This influence is usually beneficial. But, at the same time, it opens the door to apocalypse, such as nuclear wars or genetic manipulation that may degrade humanity or destroy it.

The final reason for applying ethics to science lies in its epistemological limits.[71] Science is only one of the sources of knowledge available to us. It only provides us with that part of reality that it can

70 Sophocles, *Antigone* (Gallimard, Pleiades, 1962).
71 See D. Lambert, op. cit.

discover through observation and experimentation. It says nothing about the uniqueness of people, nothing about meaning or purpose, and nothing significant about moral suffering, evil or destiny. These vital matters lie outside its sphere, but they are at the heart of our political choices and the building of our future.

Given the growing variety and complexity of the techno-sciences, it is necessary to create in firms and society places for dialogue, in which people can not only understand and debate the stakes of new discoveries and technological breakthroughs but also influence the use to which they are put and the conditions for their implementation. A new methodology is required to lead this type of dialogue and guide the choices. A dialogue between experts and those who are concerned about the significance and uses of new discoveries would help to take full advantage of them and to avoid or limit their most negative applications. It is important for society, users and social and political actors to participate in the debate, as well as representatives from various fields of human knowedge, such as philosophy, sociology, the law, religion and so on. Only a multidisciplinary approach can inform the building of the world to come.

Social innovations

Today, creativity, innovation and entrepreneurial activity have gone well beyond the scope of capitalist enterprise. Thousands of initiatives appear globally to offer innovative solutions in the social field: social entrepreneurship, solidarity economy and fair trade. They are a sign of an increasing number of more accountable entrepreneurial activities. This abundance of creativity comes up with new forms of businesses that, far from competing with more conventional structures, are an indispensable complement to them and a source of cultural inspiration. Social innovation is defined as any new initiative—products, services or models—that meets social needs more effectively than existing alternatives, and which simultaneously creates new social relationships or collaborations.[72] This approach is not only interested in the content of innovation but also in the way it is socially implemented. A major theme of this approach is to make people stand on their own two feet and to make them responsible for their own development. Social innovation not only improves the wellbeing of society, it

---

72 A. Hubert, *Empowering People, Driving Change: Social Innovation in the European Union*, A Report to the European Commission, July 2010.

strengthens its capacity for initiative and change.[73]
This concept is very broad, but the basic idea is close
to our purpose: initiative, inventiveness and creativity are the real sources of economic progress.

Social entrepreneurship has grown in recent
years, with or without the help of commercial businesses. This represents new types of entrepreneur
and innovation, and the movement aims to put the
qualities of the entrepreneur (vision, appetite for risk
and the ability to convince) at the service of priority social causes.

This new type of entrepreneur shows that it is not
only possible to give creativity a social focus, but that
it can be successful and sustainable. Innovative initiatives appear globally and in the most diverse fields.
An interesting study[74] presents 80 interesting cases in
sectors as diverse as sustainable agriculture, sustainable architecture, biodiversity, waste management,
microfinance, and renewable energy.

International associations have been created to support this new type of entrepreneur and to spread the

73 Jacques Attali thinks that a "positive economy based more
on freeness, is becoming possible thanks to the technological revolution that allows us to dedicate more time to creation and altruism".
74 S. Darnil, and M. Le Roux, *80 Hommes pour changer le
monde. Entreprendre pour la Planète* (JC Lattès, 2005).

culture. The most important of these is Ashoka, founded by Bill Drayton in India in 1980. It aims to support innovative social entrepreneurs in areas such as health, education, training, sustainable development, the fight against discrimination, human rights and so on.

Fair trade is an illustration on a global scale of a social economy. This movement was born out of motivations different to those of traditional capitalist enterprises, but still serves the market. Its purpose is to establish greater justice in competitive deals and exchanges between the poorest farmers and major players in the developed countries. To do this, they have innovated in the area of production and distribution channels and forms of financing, and in associative forms of cooperation and communication with the end consumer, including a certification system. The Max Havelaar Foundation is just one example among several. In its fight against poverty and injustice, Oxfam and its stores around the world share a similar objective.

The **solidarity economy** has developed in many areas. One of the most visible is that of food aid. In France, "Restos du cœur" and "Epiceries solidaires" are well-known examples. They are the work of true entrepreneurs and owe their success to important innovations in terms of supply, financing, organization, cooperation and partnerships. A global solidarity movement, the "Emmaus Communities" was created to fight against the causes of poverty by organizing self-help and relief to those who are suffering. This non-governmental organization (NGO) was born out of an awareness of the social responsibilities of its members in the face of injustice. One of its means of action is recovery work that can give value to any object and multiply the possibilities of emergency action to help those most in need. More recently, the example, let's say the archetype, of social innovation is the Grameen Bank, a village bank, founded by Muhammad Yunus in Bangladesh, and whose model was extended to the whole world. The idea was as follows:[75]

> Poverty is very rarely due to personal problems, laziness or a lack of intelligence but systematically to the prohibitive cost of capital, even in very small amounts... What is missing structurally is access to small capital, refundable at fairer rates and over a staggered period to fund micro-projects... So the poor will enter the economic loop and generate their own income... a quarter century later, the bank is present in 46,000 villages and has already paid more than $4.5 billion to 12 million people, 96% of whom are women.

75 See S. Darnil, and M. Le Roux, op. cit., 2005.

These social innovations give life to companies of a different kind, with a social purpose rather than profit, not dependent on the financial markets, and more participatory in their operation. They often fill a void or a gap in the current dynamics of the market economy. Nevertheless, some of them cooperate with capitalist firms that can provide them with technological, managerial or commercial know-how and financial support. They can open doors, be an example, and even encourage the adoption of social responsibilities by economic players.

Social innovations contribute to the emergence of a more responsible development model that is more focused on the "bottom of the pyramid". They can be a powerful engine because they mobilize a lot of energy, talent and capital. They undoubtedly deserve analysis and systematic evaluations to increase their effectiveness and fields of action.[76]

76 P. Kourilsky et al. (2009) FACTS Reports, founding documents: http://factsreports.revues.org.

Navigare necesse est
(Motto of the Hanseatic League)

Main works by Philippe de Woot

Pour une doctrine de l'entreprise (Paris: Seuil, 1968)

Management stratégique des groupes industriels (with Xavier Desclée) (Paris: Economica, 1984)

High Technology Europe (Oxford: Blackwell, 1989)

Le métier de dirigeant (with Olivier Lecerf) (Paris: Ed. de Fallois, 1991)

Euromanagement, A New Style for the Global Market (with Roland Calori and Hélène Bloom) (London: Kogan Page, 1994)

Méditation sur le Pouvoir (Louvain la Neuve: De Boeck, 1998)

Les défis de la globalisation: Babel ou Pentecôte? (with Jacques Delcourt) (Presses universitaires de Louvain, 2001)

Should Prometheus Be Bound? Corporate Global Responsibility (Basingstoke and New York, Palgrave Macmillan, 2005)

Lettre ouverte aux dirigeants chrétiens en temps d'urgence (Paris, Lethielleux-Desclée de Brouwer, 2009)

Repenser l'entreprise (Brussells: Académie Royale de Belgique, 2013)

Spirituality and Business. A Christian Viewpoint (GSE Research Ltd, 2013)

Rethinking the Enterprise (Greenleaf Publishing, 2014)

An environmentally friendly book printed and bound in England by www.printondemand-worldwide.com